What Our Readers Have Said...

"Although I consider myself a seasoned sales professional, it is helpful to have past learning's refreshed. The books were also beneficial because of the information concerning 'trends' in the sales relationship. The sales process should be viewed as dynamic since business relationships change regularly."

•

"For the particular business I am in and the type of sales calls I have, I find that the books in the Pinpoint Sales Training Series are very often applicable to how I conduct business. I would recommend them to other sales people, just not ones that are in my industry."

•

"These books provide very good concepts. It fits in well with the Bell Leadership training program that I attended in November."

•

"I use this material in these books and apply it to my customers and other employees I work with."

•

"I would like to know other topics. Is there anything on Production Management or Consultative Selling or Time Management?"

•

"These books are great tools that should be used as guidelines for our everyday

supervisory practices. You need to take the time to do a short self-evaluation when reading them."

•

"The Pinpoint Training Series delivers information that could be used in a lot different areas."

•

"I like this because I can take them with me to read at a convenient time. I feel the little time I have to spend in the office is best use on activities that directly relate to revenue opportunities. I like the short amount of time it takes to keep up with these."

•

"I prefer the self-study approach; it fits in with my schedule."

•

"My thought is that the real value of these books comes into effect when doing the action plans."

•

"Short and sweet. These books are easy to comprehend."

•

"I have enjoyed reading these books. They are relevant to today's work environment and the ongoing change in the way we manage our workforce."

•

"I do feel that these books have been very helpful to me at my job."

•

"I think a lot of the recommendations in these books are very useful, and can be applicable to everyday situations. If nothing else, it's a good reference guide to fall back upon if a situation arises in the future."

•

"These books are relevant to today's work environment and the ongoing change in the way we manage our workforce."

•

Difficult Customer Behaviors

Pinpoint Sales Skill Development Training Series

TIMOTHY F. BEDNARZ

MAJORIUM
BUSINESS PRESS

Pinpoint Sales Skill Development Training Series
"Difficult Customer Behaviors"
Timothy F. Bednarz

Graphic design: Monika Pawlak

Majorium Business Press
2025 Main Street
Stevens Point, WI 54481
715.342.1018 • 800.654.4935

ISBN 978-1-882181-92-6

Printed in the United States of America

Introduction

The Pinpoint Sales Skill Development Training Series is designed for targeted training and education regarding increased improvement in a specific skill or competency.

Each book within this series is designed to be easy to use, understand and apply to your job. It can be used as a basis for training individuals, as a discussion guide or as a personal training tool.

Each chapter within this book discusses a specific concept. When you have completed all eight chapters you should have a 360° perspective of the topic.

Additionally, each chapter is divided into specific sections:

- The first section provides you with an overview of the topic
- The Implications section discusses why the concept is important, and why it is important to learn and apply.
- The Strategies, Tips & Techniques to Apply section teaches how to use and apply the particular concept to your work.
- The Points to Ponder section gives you something to think about or to be discussed with a group setting. These are questions not meant to be immediately answered, but to be pondered over time.
- The Training Activity section provides you with the tools to transfer what you have learned to your job. It is designed to help create an action plan to effectively apply the concept.

Each of the topics in this series is time-tested and proven in the marketplace. They have been used by thousands of employees as training tools. Many of the users have commented that what made these books valuable, was the ability to refer to them when a problem surfaced. They indicated that they remembered reading about the exact problem. They referred back to these books and found an appropriate solution.

You will find them equally valuable as a resource in your professional development library.

Table of Contents

LEARNING OBJECTIVES:

- To identify negative customer behaviors.
- The motivations behind game playing.
- How to sell to difficult personality types.
- To deal with a host of customer problems.

1

Learn to Identify and Understand Negative Customer Behavior

Just as customers come in all shapes and sizes, so do personal behaviors and personalities. It is the main role of salespeople to keep potential customers interested in the services or products they offer. In order to do this, they must be able to relate to them on a personal level and become fully aware of their individual expectations, desires, internal thoughts and influences.

IMPLICATIONS – WHAT THIS MEANS TO YOU

Effectively solving customer problems and meeting specific requirements rests heavily upon understanding how and why salespeople are being challenged during selling encounters. Challenges should most often not be taken personally. They are simply a way for some potential customers to seek out more information prior to purchasing, and determine how far they feel they can trust salespeople to fill their particular requirements in a timely and honest fashion. Winning sales often depends upon appropriate responses that only come from understanding individual behaviors, motives, curiosity and feelings as well as potential buyers' underlying thoughts and interests.

STRATEGIES, TIPS & TECHNIQUES TO APPLY

The most difficult types of potential buyers to please are those who tend to challenge everything salespeople say or do. Yet, in today's marketplace the need to surmount their various challenges is becoming far more paramount. Salespeople may begin to feel threatened, thinking that there is no hope to win such prospects over and no chance of securing their sales. However if they succumb to believing that these potential customers' actions are strictly the result of negative behaviors, it is easy to think it is useless to try to deal with them. Many salespeople end up walking away from possible sales, rather than dealing with various types of negative behaviors and challenges in order to win them.

Rather than walking away from potential customers, the following suggestions may help overcome certain behavior-related sales challenges.

Salespeople should:

- Respond professionally, not react personally. It is important not to let emotions rule and control the sales process. This only leads to asking for negative behaviors to surface.
- Respond to issues, not challenges. This is an effective way for salespeople to avoid feeling they are being challenged, and to think and act clearly and unemotionally.
- Maintain the stance of being non-defensive and non-offensive. This works to reduce conflict, which otherwise tends to bring negative behaviors to the surface. Some potential buyers feel personally threatened or annoyed when salespeople appear to be "on the defensive" and reacting emotionally to their challenges and comments.
- Do not display a sense of rejection. This tends to signal some potential buyers that they can apply negative behaviors as a means to control the selling process and gain concessions or favors.
- Stay decisive, but if unsure about something, say so without fear. Assure potential customers that there will be an answer "ASAP." Quick responses establish professional credibility. A lack of profes-

sional credibility by numerous other salespeople is one reason why negative behaviors tend to exist.

- Remember that they are not obligated to solve any problems not directly related to their intended selling purpose. If salespeople do choose to help resolve or make suggestions regarding other business-related issues, they should make certain to let the prospect know that it is a service they tend to provide only on a selective basis, and because they understand that they are serious in their intentions to purchase. This action will often discourage prospects from challenging any further, and will generally break through existing barriers to moving the sales processes forward.
- Never appear deceptive. Keep responses clear, direct and straightforward. Being open and honest works well to inhibit the use of negative behaviors since it generally overcomes feeling the need to apply them. It also works to emphasize that salespeople choose to maintain high ethical standards and associated actions to sustain them.

POINTS TO PONDER — SOMETHING TO THINK ABOUT

1. When you review your customer base in its entirety, have you experienced an increase in overall negative or challenging attitudes? If so, why do you think this is occurring? Explain.
2. What is your response to encounters with negative customer behaviors? How does it affect your sales motivation and persistence?

TRAINING ACTIVITY — APPLICATION & ACTION PLAN

Determine if certain behaviors are used to gain more information or to develop reasons for justifying the purchase of your products or services.

1. Determine certain behaviors that tend to signal an interest in your product or service.
2. What specific behaviors have you observed when potential buyers generally want to gain more information about what you are offering?
3. Create a list of negative behaviors you encounter that pose a serious threat to wanting to deal with the prospective buyers using them.
4. After listing these behaviors, try to identify why they were used. Jot down two strategies that can be used to overcome each of them.

2

Motivations Behind Game Playing

One of the realities of selling is dealing with prospects who tend to play games or continually play "hot and cold" in relation to the selling process. Salespeople need to understand the real motivations behind the games prospects tend to play. Motivational factors generally apply to both retail and business-to-business situations. The first signs that games are in progress come from the active use of "procrastination" or "objection" techniques.

The bottom line is to be prepared for these situations. An active defense comes from developing the product, competitive and customer knowledge needed to approach accounts from a position of strength and value.

Salespeople also need to be alert to what is happening within sales encounters. Being able to identify why prospects succumb to game-playing tactics is essential. Oftentimes it is because their curiosity and interest have not been sparked to the point where they take selling situations seriously. Therefore it is essential to initially uncover their true needs, motivations and expectations and use them in a way to gain their full attention. Once a sincere interest is established, game-playing tactics are generally minimized or eliminated.

IMPLICATIONS – WHAT THIS MEANS TO YOU

Game playing is often a red flag that indicates particular sales processes are not going well. Salespeople must be able to quickly identify the causes behind why they are not moving smoothly along, and determine appropriate responses to recover an interest in what they are presenting and discussing. Sometimes this will become impossible and the best response is to simply close a particular conversation or encounter, and move on.

Game playing often goes beyond prospects voicing objections and stalls. It can be a way of saying that certain sales are simply not going to transpire. Many prospects tend to go to great lengths to protect their self-interests, and game playing is often a creative way to do it. It is up to salespeople to "read between the lines" and understand what is really happening.

STRATEGIES, TIPS & TECHNIQUES TO APPLY

There can be many motivational factors that underscore reasons behind sales-related game playing, which often include:

Affordability

A need for particular product or service offerings may exist, but the reasons behind not wanting to become involved in the sales process that leads to their purchase can be due to the fact that certain prospects simply cannot afford them. Perhaps they do not have the necessary credit and cannot arrange for financing nor do they have the funds or cash flow to afford updates or necessary improvements to effectively incorporate newer products or services. This is a common problem with many smaller companies, but it has been creeping into larger ones as well, as budget constraints become more of the norm than the exception.

When prospects are facing this reality, some will tend to use "face-saving" techniques to protect their egos and business reputations. Normally they will begin to play games in order to string out the process in hopes that salespeople will eventually go away.

The only way to counter this situation is to make sure that prospects are carefully qualified before investing a great deal of time in working their accounts. If certain prospects cannot afford particular products or services, it is better to allow them to "save face," which ultimately helps in the end to save salespeople's time and energy, as well as prevent increased amounts of frustration. It is far more effective at times to quietly walk away from certain sales situations, and then follow up occasionally to determine whether circumstances have changed.

Egos

The ego factor can take many forms in game-playing sales situations. As in the situation described above, prospects simply cannot afford particular products or services at any price and are often too embarrassed to tell salespeople the truth about their situation.

In other circumstances, some individuals might have represented themselves as the decision maker, while in reality they have no authority to make purchases. They have gone too far down the road under this representation, do not know how to get out of the situation they have placed themselves into, and begin to use game-playing tactics to prevent themselves from having to disclose the truth.

On the opposite end of the spectrum are individuals who need to prove their superiority. These prospects generally tend to have inferiority complexes. Because salespeople may appear better dressed, make more money or work for a more prestigious company than they do, prospects may feel the need to prove their superiority over them. Many of these prospects play control games in order to gain a feeling of self-worth.

Inability to Say 'No'

Some prospects may like particular sales offerings, but have no real reasons or need to purchase them. The problem is that they do not know how to say "no," or feel they cannot handle the pressure salespeople might place on them if they do.

The sole purpose of these prospects' game-playing strategies is to string salespeople along to the point of complete frustration, hoping they will just go away. It is important that salespeople employ techniques to probe and determine the true motivation behind their actions, because having no need for particular offerings simply wastes their time and energy that could be better spent with other prospects that may have a legitimate interest in what they have to offer.

Control

Ego and control go hand in hand. However, some prospects are motivated by their ability to control not only the particular sales situations they find themselves in, but also the salespeople selling to them. They feel the need to play control games in order to gain an upper hand, increase their feelings of superiority, or simply make salespeople grovel for their business. Underneath it all, some prospects make salespeople's lives miserable purely for their own entertainment. They misuse their authority and power to increase their own personal feelings of control over others.

The best strategy in controlling game-playing situations is to approach prospects from a non-confrontational position. It is better to elevate these types of prospects to being experts in their own field, while working to draw out their ability to help solve complex problems and define workable and effective solutions. In so doing salespeople can better align themselves with these "controlling" types of individuals.

If salespeople resort to taking a pure sales posture where they project themselves as being experts and in control, they are in a much weaker position to deal with these types of prospects. They also become highly susceptible to having to deal with their control games.

POINTS TO PONDER – SOMETHING TO THINK ABOUT

1. What are some of the games you have encountered in certain sales situations? What happened and what did you do to defeat the game playing? Explain.
2. Do some of the motivations discussed above describe current situations you find yourself in? Explain how you might resolve some game-playing techniques with the knowledge you just learned.

TRAINING ACTIVITY — APPLICATION & ACTION PLAN

Being able to identify why prospects succumb to game playing tactics is essential. In order to help identify motivational factors, use previous selling situations to identify the various types of actions that had their roots in game playing that centered around:

- Affordability
- A prospect's ego
- A particular prospect's inability to say "no"
- Control issues

3

Breaking the Grip of Irrational Loyalty

All salespeople have prospects, often major potential accounts, who are so comfortable with the competition that they won't even consider making a switch. Their loyalty may appear irrational and remain intact even when they are presented with compelling reasons to make a change.

IMPLICATIONS — WHAT THIS MEANS TO YOU

Virtually every salesman and woman has at least one major prospective account in this category. It is a frustrating situation: the buyer doesn't want to consider any alternatives, however superior, and the salesperson's only course of action seems to be a direct frontal attack on the competition. However, due to the prospect being a staunch advocate for the competition, any such attack will be viewed dimly. Consequently, most salespeople tend to wait out these accounts, awaiting a change in decision makers, or they may attempt to get a small trial order to crack the account.

STRATEGIES, TIPS & TECHNIQUES TO APPLY

Salespeople lumping their products and services with the competition's is an effective means of breaking their grip on a potential account. Once done, they can show their compatibility and how they work well together. At this point a level playing field is established and the prospect can agree that both products are equal.

This agreement can be leveraged by introducing a problem the prospect agrees they are likely to face, one the salesperson knows only their product can solve. They then demonstrate how only their product, with an exclusive feature the competitive product doesn't have, can solve it.

The benefits of solving this problem, including downtime avoided and increased efficiency, should be quantified so the prospect is able to place an actual value on the solution.

In this way the competition can actually be favorably commented on, thereby not placing the buyer on the defensive, while clearly demonstrating the superiority and value the salesperson's product can deliver.

By introducing a problem the competition is unable to solve, the salesperson is positioned above and beyond the rest of the competitors and is able to break the grip on irrational loyalty.

POINTS TO PONDER — SOMETHING TO THINK ABOUT

1. What has been your sales approach when you have encountered a prospect with irrational loyalty to the competition? Explain.
2. Without badmouthing the competition, what tactics to counter their actions are you able to take? Explain.

TRAINING ACTIVITY — APPLICATION & ACTION PLAN

Identify a prospect with irrational loyalty toward a competitor that you are unable to break.

1. Lump your products with those of the competitor and demonstrate that they are equal.
2. Identify a problem your product can solve that the competitions cannot.
3. Quantify the benefits of using your product to solve that problem.
4. Create a sales approach based upon this information to crack the account.

4

Selling to an Abrasive Buyer

Salespeople must continually sell to and deal with abrasive customer personalities. Some are inherently abrupt and short in their responses because it is just part of their nature. Many times abrasiveness or abruptness can simply be a front to cope with or manage various sales situations. In either case, from a professional standpoint, these types of buyers can be extremely difficult to handle and sell to.

There are circumstances when abrasive individuals are placed into purchasing positions for particular reasons. Some companies want to develop reputations as being tough negotiators. In other cases certain types of more unemotional individuals are better for dealing with a host of salespeople on a daily basis, or for prolonged periods of time. In still other instances, some companies use abrasive individuals to weed out applicable from unusable vendor offerings. In all cases and circumstances, these types of individuals pose major sales challenges.

IMPLICATIONS — WHAT THIS MEANS TO YOU

Abrasive buyers tend to set their own agendas and use intimidation and tactless behavior to their advantage. They are generally superb manipulators who often get what they want. Abrasive individuals can bully salespeople, which results in them losing their focus or fumbling through their presentations, making them appear unprofessional and unprepared and reducing the perceived value of their offering.

It is important to keep in mind that abrasive and bullying techniques are oftentimes used for the primary purpose of creating favorable negotiating positions. This technique generally works quite effectively unless it is recognized and countered.

It is important for salespeople to understand that abrasive personality use is often an applied buying technique, which should not be mistaken for a character flaw. When salespeople understand the "rules of the game" as specified by the types of buyers using this manipulative method, they can maneuver in a way that works to their own advantage. However, it takes personal experience with these kinds of individuals before effective countering techniques can be polished. The stress and intimidation initially faced by salespeople can be daunting, but it is imperative that they learn how to effectively deal with these types of sales situations.

STRATEGIES, TIPS & TECHNIQUES TO APPLY

Various types of abrasive behaviors are used to control the sales process. Abruptness that suggests annoyance and lack of interest can be an attempt by certain buyers to obtain more favorable company concessions or discounts. Other buyers will employ abrasive behaviors because they want to "shine" and look good for their superiors. In other circumstances some are mandated to exhibit abrasive behaviors and callous attitudes toward salespeople as a way to limit vendors from continually calling and barraging them with various promotions or specials.

The following tactics can be very effective when dealing with callous and abrasive buyers:

Redirecting

When abrasive buyers begin to throw a curve at salespeople, the best action to take is to defuse their negative or tactless remarks by redirecting particular comments to the next point in the sales discussion.

Keep It Light

Humor is an effective way for salespeople to defuse abrasive behaviors. Making light of an abrasive remark or behavior can often work to reduce or deflect personal attacks. When salespeople use humor they are generally able to immediately change the subject in a non-threatening way. This tends to catch most buyers off guard and often minimizes additional abusive behaviors.

Inserting Emotion

It may be necessary for salespeople to get "intentionally emotional" with certain abrasive buyers. The key is to keep actual emotions under control while openly demonstrating an outward type of surprised or painful response. This may cause some abusive buyers to back off, which also makes them more aware that their actions have consequences.

Timing

Salespeople should note the timing of abrasive outbreaks. Often used as positioning techniques to keep salespeople off balance, most negative comments, innuendos and demands will come in waves. Once particular patterns are identified, the key is to inject essential sales points that stimulate a sense of interest and curiosity and reserve others that are less powerful for later discussions.

It is essential to maintain a structured sales approach in situations where negative behaviors are being used. The need for prospects to terminate certain sales discussions and meetings is not unusual and should be expected. It may frustrate salespeople, since they will be unable to complete their calls or move them immediately ahead, but it does not necessarily imply the sale is lost. In some cases this action is simply part of the overall negotiating strategy, where particular buyers expect to return to the sales process to readdress offerings at a later time.

Closing Strategies

When dealing with abusive and abrasive buyers, salespeople need to concentrate on their actual closing strategies. Remembering that these behavioral tactics are often used as a means to set the stage for better negotiating terms and positioning, it is essential to convince these buyers that the best deal has been negotiated and anything further crosses the line of realistic expectations. Since this is a counter positioning stance, salespeople should allow the involved buyers to make the next move.

Concessions should be saved for the end of negotiations, thus allowing salespeople to make buyers look good in the eyes of their superiors. This also aids in ending all negotiating sessions with a lasting favorable impression.

POINTS TO PONDER — SOMETHING TO THINK ABOUT

1. How often do you encounter abrasive buyers? Do you consider their behavior to be a character flaw or a tactic?
2. What has been your typical response to an abrasive or callous buyer?

TRAINING ACTIVITY — APPLICATION & ACTION PLAN

Analyze and resolve the following situations:

1. An abrasive buyer states that his or her business will be terminated if you do not agree to an important concession. What responses would help keep both your respect as a professional and the account?
2. An abrasive buyer takes control of the sales encounter in a hostile way when talking on the phone. The same individual has responded this way in a previous call. What can you do to prevent the situation from happening again?

5

Disagreeable Prospects

Some prospects can be totally disagreeable and object to everything salespeople present, discuss and do. While there are individuals who do find fault with everything and everyone for no apparent reason, there may be a "method to their madness." Many disagreeable prospects may be using unpleasant, complaining and oftentimes alienating behavior as an underlying negotiating tactic.

IMPLICATIONS – WHAT THIS MEANS TO YOU

In some sales encounters prospective buyers may begin to repeatedly complain about perceived weaknesses in particular product offerings. They blow these perceived weaknesses out of proportion in a bid to force salespeople to accept their complaints as legitimate and control the direction of the sales process. If salespeople succumb to agreeing that these prospects' complaints are valid, their offerings are immediately devalued. Doing this gives prospects not only control over the entire selling process, but also a major advantage when it comes to negotiating their purchases.

It is essential for salespeople to understand that these types of prospects are generally very skilled at using various types of complaining or belittling techniques to their advantage. Salespeople must exercise a great deal of patience, wisdom and control to resist their manipulative efforts. In essence, many disagreeable prospects seek to use salespeople's good natures and their tendencies to please and be of service to their personal benefit.

STRATEGIES, TIPS & TECHNIQUES TO APPLY

Disagreeable prospects can be devious and must be handled carefully. Salespeople need to be aware of the potential pitfalls and guard against being taken off guard, detoured in their focus and direction, and placed on the defensive. When salespeople fall into this trap, the tendency is to make immediate concessions to overcome their complaints and secure the sale, which is precisely the prospect's intent.

Proper qualification procedures and the careful development of sales relationships are paramount in these situations. Salespeople that are in a hurry to move the sales process along to overcome stalls, objections and complaints are likely to make more concessions than needed and expected. Those who take the time to properly qualify their prospects and put forth extra effort to get to know them better are less likely to go down this unproductive path.

It is important to separate legitimate complaints and objections from those designed to place salespeople on the defensive. Prospects who complain about details and specifics tend to be perfectionists who use their objections as a way to define their personal expectations. With these types of prospects, salespeople need to take extreme care to address major and minor points in their conversations and presentations, making certain all facts presented are fully substantiated and verified.

Salespeople should use care and caution when dealing with prospects that tend to pinpoint weaknesses or complain about how particular functions, features or applications will not be able to realistically benefit their company or meet their needs. Rather than validate complaints, negative reactions and reasoning, salespeople should acknowledge them and probe for specific functions, features or properties that prospects feel are lacking. It is imperative to determine the needs such prospects feel are not being met and craft solutions to resolve their complaints.

Salespeople must recognize that there will always be prospective buyers who tend to be pessimistic about everything and that, in the end, there may be no way to please them. Once they determine that particular product offerings appear to be aligned with the prospect's general needs and requirements, yet there is a failure to respond positively to the offerings, there are several options. Salespeople can:

- Walk away from the prospect
- Continue to develop the account and identify problems to address
- Attempt to work around the particular prospect

If the initial qualification process indicates that there are other influencers and decision makers that can be possibly accessed, salespeople may be better served to deal with these individuals. It is also possible that some initially disagreeable prospects can become resources for the names and positions of others who would be more interested in further discussing the particular offerings.

POINTS TO PONDER – SOMETHING TO THINK ABOUT

1. Have you ever fallen into a "complaining trap"? What lessons have you learned?
2. What has been your personal method of dealing with disagreeable prospects?

TRAINING ACTIVITY – APPLICATION & ACTION PLAN

There is a difference between genuinely pessimistic prospects and ones who attempt to use complaints to their advantage.

1. Detail the differences between the two.
2. Develop strategies to counter both types of prospects and ways to address the various accompanying behaviors.

6

Handling the Reluctant Buyer

Many salespeople target prospects that stall or flatly refuse to do business with them. As nothing appears to instill any level of interest or break through the selling barriers that exist, working with these types of individuals becomes a continual source of frustration.

IMPLICATIONS — WHAT THIS MEANS TO YOU

Certain prospects have mastered the art of saying "no." They often ask for written proposals, take an interest in and listen to formal sales presentations, and even ask a series of leading questions, all of which are positive signs that they are interested in the salesperson's offerings. Yet they never get to the point of actively moving the sales process ahead or making any commitment to purchase. Salespeople can alter their selling strategies and approaches without gaining any type of workable advantage. The only thing they seem to accomplish is wasting a great deal of time preparing meaningless proposals and presentations.

Salespeople are challenged to handle reluctant prospects in a way that limits the wasting of their time and resources while still keeping the possibility of doing business with them open. Walking away from these prospective accounts is the last thing salespeople should think about doing, since things do have a tendency to change over time. New opportunities may present themselves, or reluctant buyers may leave and be replaced with other more accommodating individuals.

STRATEGIES, TIPS & TECHNIQUES TO APPLY

Rather than increase individual frustrations, there are several strategies salespeople can use to keep reluctant prospects "in the system" while minimizing wasted time, effort and resources. These include:

Assign Them a Low Priority

For obvious reasons, reluctant prospects should not be assigned a high selling priority. While they are worthy of continued contact, they are not worth high levels of attention. Occasional contact may be all that is required to determine whether or not circumstances have changed. As long as salespeople continue to call upon them, the possibility of doing business remains intact.

Give Them Control

Since past histories generally reflect a resistance to do business or work through the sales process to its completion, salespeople should let reluctant prospects take control of the selling situation. Once initial conversations are initiated, salespeople should allow them to make the next move or pose the next topic of discussion, thus sending the signal they may be serious about beginning an established sales relationship. This does not mean that salespeople should attempt to contact them on a consistent basis if they are cut short. Even when return encounters or calls occur, salespeople should proceed cautiously, especially when certain prospects have asked for proposals in the past without any effective results afterward.

Continue Building Trust and Rapport

As salespeople continue contacting reluctant prospects, their main objective should be to build rapport and buyer confidence. An emphasis should be placed on selling their professionalism and expertise. With these types of individuals, salespeople may be better served making contact in person rather than over the phone or by email. The personal approach is often more beneficial for building secure business relationships. Personal meetings also allow salespeople to continue collecting information and data about particular needs and requirements in order to develop insight as to why a reluctance to do business with them exists.

Get in or Let It Go

Developing a strategy to get in these prospects' doors should become a top priority. When finally presented with an opportunity to sell, salespeople should present sufficient information and specific material to spark an interest and to make informed decisions easier and quicker. They should keep past prospect histories in mind and take certain sales processes not progressing as a signal not to exert any further time imparting information or making concessions. This may result in certain reluctant prospects giving their business to a competitor, but it is likely this was their original intent anyway.

Stay on Their Vendor List

Salespeople should never give up on reluctant prospects or on securing any sales from their respective companies. Circumstances change, and fresh selling opportunities can easily become available. It is essential for salespeople to keep bridges intact by remaining positive, staying in touch with prospective accounts and continually working to position themselves to be able to take full advantage of any resulting transformations and positive changes.

POINTS TO PONDER – SOMETHING TO THINK ABOUT

1. When you experience a sale going nowhere, how do you normally handle the situation?
2. What is your typical approach to prospects that refuse to do business with you? Explain.

TRAINING ACTIVITY – APPLICATION & ACTION PLAN

List on a sheet of paper the prospects that have continually refused to do business with you.

1. Outline the specific strategies and approaches you have used with each of them.
2. Analyze your activities and techniques to determine whether any have proved positive in your repeated efforts to work the particular accounts.
3. What lessons can be derived from your analysis? Identify strategies you can use in the future to effectively handle various types of reluctant prospects. Determine techniques that are able to instill a real and immediate interest in your particular sales offering.

7

Dealing with Customer Problems

Coping with ongoing selling-related difficulties is a way of life for most salespeople. They just seem to come with the profession. The causes of many problems are quite often out of salespeople's direct control, but it becomes their responsibility to resolve them anyway.

As problems create a critical juncture in the relationship process with most customers, it is essential that salespeople's responses are quick, decisive and thorough. How and when problems are resolved will generally determine the nature of all future dealings with the people involved.

Even though salespeople may not be directly related to the cause, it is not unusual for customers to vent their frustration over problems on the representatives from whom they bought the products or services.

For instance, in one such situation a woman came into a flooring store and bitterly complained about the poor quality of the carpet she purchased and the accompanying installation.

After much heated discussion it was revealed that the woman had initially purchased the carpeting at a discount outlet and had it in stalled by a local handy man, but she choose to complain to the client because his establishment was the major local distributor for the name brand she purchased. Not even a legitimate customer, she nevertheless felt compelled to come into the establishment and make a public scene about the products and services in front of other potential customers.

Unfortunately, this is not an isolated incident, and there are many other types of situations where similar circumstances occur.

IMPLICATIONS – WHAT THIS MEANS TO YOU

Right or wrong, salespeople are often on the receiving end of customer venting, anger and hostility. Whether or not it is legitimately their problem to solve, customers often make it their problem, and they expect immediate attention and a readily available solution.

In the incident cited above, the retailer calmed the woman down, examined the facts, inspected her problem and ultimately sold her new carpeting and installation. This turned an angry individual into a happy customer.

Salespeople must remember that complaints are golden opportunities. Studies have shown that less than 4% of unhappy customers actually make a point to complain. The rest simply find new suppliers. When a complaint needs addressing, salespeople have a high likelihood of maintaining the business account or gaining a new one if they respond quickly and professionally. Studies indicate delayed or inappropriate responses can become extremely costly and are able to produce all types of negative repercussions.

STRATEGIES, TIPS & TECHNIQUES TO APPLY

Following is a simple yet proven approach to solving most customer problems:

Identify the Core Issue

The customer will no doubt attempt to relate the problem to the salesperson. Because many complaints are symptomatic of a larger and more complicated problem, or point to other unresolved issues, salespeople should probe further in order to define the real problem.

Qualify and Quantify the Problem

Salespeople should determine whether the problem is the company's responsibility or the customer's, then quantify the problem by defining its size and scope and the impact the problem directly has on the individual customer or a customer's business.

Explore the Problem

Salespeople should identify the root causes of the problem within their company. Did late delivery, manufacturing defects, faulty materials, lack of customer education, or another issue cause or contribute to this problem?

Resolve and Report the Problem

Once causes have been identified, salespeople should solve the problem to the customer's satisfaction, then report their findings to senior management so that its causes can be acknowledged and actions taken to eliminate possible recurrences of the same issue in the future.

POINTS TO PONDER – SOMETHING TO THINK ABOUT

1. Have you encountered customers who complained about problems that were not your responsibility to resolve? What did you do?
2. What types of problems are you faced with most often? Are there some strategies to resolve them that appear to work better than others? If so, why?

TRAINING ACTIVITY — APPLICATION & ACTION PLAN

1. Develop responses, comments and step-by-step strategies that work to address and resolve common problems.
2. Make certain that particular responses and comments simultaneously work to calm upset customers.
3. Prepare them on various note cards for reference.
4. Create a checklist of the points listed within this lesson.
5. Keep a copy with you at all times and use the points listed to work through and resolve the next customer problem you encounter.

8

Positioning Yourself in the Prospect's Mind

Technology has generally forced many products into a commodity status where almost all of the key features between competitive offerings are essentially the same. Under this scenario, big sales can often hinge on relatively minor differences.

Salespeople must invest time with individual prospects to determine their real requirements that generally necessitate purchasing particular products or services. This should include a list of the "must" and "nice to have" features of particular product or service offerings. The determination of real and specific requirements should always be a part of the initial qualification process.

A successfully positioned offering should include all of the "must" features and as many of the "nice to have" features that can be successfully matched to secondary priorities. The offering should try to include at least two "nice to have" features in order to spark higher levels of interest.

IMPLICATIONS — WHAT THIS MEANS TO YOU

When salespeople position themselves in such a way that their presented offerings appear to be "just like all the others," they are placed at a serious disadvantage. They are unable to provide prospects with a real or distinct reason to buy. If salespeople are to get any sales, they are oftentimes leveraged so tightly against competitors that they are forced to discount their prices to secure them. This is because prospects do not perceive any enhanced value in what is being sold.

STRATEGIES, TIPS & TECHNIQUES TO APPLY

Salespeople need to develop a clear understanding of just who their competition is, what their products and services are, and their accompanying features and benefits. In most sales situations, purchases will be decided among no more than two or three primary competitive offerings.

It is essential to develop a clear understanding of competitive offerings strengths and weaknesses. This allows salespeople to leverage their own particular product strengths, as well as company-related advantages that work to position themselves more favorably in prospects' minds.

By thoroughly qualifying prospective buyers in order to fully define "must" and "nice to have" features, salespeople are better able to establish inherent value and monetary savings in regard to their particular offerings. This essentially creates product space and differentiation. The technique works to create favorable perceptions and impressions in the minds of most prospects.

Salespeople must be able to establish clear reasons why prospects would be better served to buy from them and not the competition. They must be able to clearly demonstrate the inherent value and enhanced benefits and detail why they can only be found in their particular offerings. If they fall short in establishing significant value and demonstrating visible differentiation, potential business can be swept away by other salespeople who are better able to convince prospects of their product or service uniqueness and money saving value.

POINTS TO PONDER – SOMETHING TO THINK ABOUT

1. How do you position yourself against the competition?
2. How are you able to successfully communicate this to the prospect?

TRAINING ACTIVITY – APPLICATION & ACTION PLAN

Take the time to collect all the information you can on particular competitive offerings.

1. Determine their product and service strengths and weaknesses.
2. Compare and contrast them against your own particular offerings.
3. Establish reasons why your company can offer advantages over competitive offerings.
4. Determine ways to effectively incorporate the information for emphasizing these advantages during initial sales discussions and throughout the sales process.
5. Develop a chart that can be referred to, which visibly demonstrates and details the differences in order to better position yourself and separate your particular offering from the competition's.

About the Author

Timothy F. Bednarz, Ph.D. is CEO of the American Management Development Group, Inc. For over 20 years he has researched, designed and authored hundreds of learning and development programs used by Fortune 1000 companies.

He is also the author of *Great! What Makes Leaders Great. What They Did, How They Did It and What You Can Learn from It* (2011).

Speaking Availability

Timothy F. Bednarz, Ph.D. is available for speaking engagements for your next meeting or association event. He can be contacted at 800-654-4935 or by e-mail at timothy.bednarz@majorium.com.

Bulk Sales

Bulk sales of this book or any other titles available from Majorium Business Press. Inquiries can be directed to sales@majorium.com, or by phone at 800-6654-4935.

Quick Order Form

Fax orders: 715-342-1118. Send this form.

Telephone orders: Call 800-654-4935 toll-free. Have your credit card ready.

Email orders: sales@majorium.com

Postal orders: Majorium Business Press, 2025 Main Street, Stevens Point, WI 54481, USA.

Please send the following books:

____

____

____

____

Please send more FREE information on:

❑Catalog ❑Speaking/Seminars ❑Mailing Lists ❑Consulting

Name: ____________________________________

Address: __________________________________

City: ____________________ State: _____ Zip: __________

Telephone: ________________________________

Email address: ______________________________

Sales tax: Please add 5.5% for products shipped to Wisconsin addresses.

Shipping by air:

United States: $4.00 for first book and $2.00 for each additional product.

International: $9.00 for first book; $5.00 for each additional product (estimate).

Made in United States
Cleveland, OH
06 November 2026

47678355R10026